YOUR POWER & AUTHORITY IN THE MAKING

A 30 DAY DEVOTIONAL
LUCIA M. CLABORN

ISBN Paperback 978-0-578-28281-7
eBook 979-8-9860477-1-3

Your Power & Authority In The Making - A 30 Day Devotional
By Lucia M. Claborn
Copyright © 2022 by Lucia M. Claborn
All rights reserved. This book or any portion thereof may not be reproduced or used in any manner whatsoever without the expressed written permission of the author.
Published in the United States of America.
Lucia Claborn, LLC
2586 County Road 165
Moulton, Alabama 35650
www.LuciaClaborn.com

All scriptures are taken from the Passion Translation unless otherwise noted.

Scripture quotations marked TPT are from The Passion Translation®. Copyright © 2017, 2018 by Passion & Fire Ministries, Inc. Used by permission. All rights reserved. www.ThePassionTranslation.com.

Holy Bible, New Living Translation, copyright © 1996, 2004, 2015 by Tyndale House Foundation. Used by permission of Tyndale House Publishers, Inc., Carol Stream, Illinois 60188. All rights reserved.

Dedication

This devotional is lovingly dedicated to you.

As you read through the pages of this devotional, my prayer is that you will renew your mind with God's Word, ponder on the thoughts, answer the questions, and receive a greater revelation that God has created you to walk in His power and authority here on earth to defeat Satan and his works.

God created you and loves you. He desires to have a personal, intimate relationship with you through daily conversations. He has greater levels of victory on His mind for you to enjoy and experience in your life today as you walk in your power and authority.

Never doubt God's mighty power to work in you and accomplish all this. He will achieve infinitely more than your greatest request, your most unbelievable dream, and exceed your wildest imagination! He will outdo them all, for his miraculous power constantly energizes you. - Ephesians 3:20

Table of Contents

Acknowledgments ix
Introduction xi
Day 1 Made In God's Image 1
Day 2 You Have Binding Power 3
Day 3 You Have a Spirit of Power 5
Day 4 Walking In Your Authority 7
Day 5 You Have All Authority 9
Day 6 Your Belief Causes Miracles 11
Day 7 Jesus Gives You His Authority 13
Day 8 You Have Imparted Authority 15
Day 9 Your Glorious Inheritance 17
Day 10 You Are Forever Alive 19
Day 11 Heirs of God Himself 21
Day 12 Stand Up To The Devil 23
Day 13 You Have Spiritual Blessings 25
Day 14 Stand Victorious In His Power 27
Day 15 You Are Destined For Victory 29
Day 16 Be Strong And Courageous 31
Day 17 Satan Is Stripped Of Authority 33
Day 18 I Have God's Resurrection Power 35
Day 19 Your Mighty Spiritual Weapons 37
Day 20 Your Miracle-Working Power 39
Day 21 Remain Alert – Stand Strong 41
Day 22 You Reign As A King 43
Day 23 God's Power Flows Through Faith 45
Day 24 Your Authority Is In Jesus 47
Day 25 Raised And Seated With Jesus 49
Day 26 God Has Given You Authority 51
Day 27 Use Your Power, Not Just Words 53
Day 28 Supernatural Explosive Power 55
Day 29 God's Miraculous Energizing Power 57
Day 30 As Jesus Is – So Am I 59
Prayer of Salvation 62
About Lucia M. Claborn 64
Other Products Available From Lucia M. Claborn 66

Acknowledgments

Creating projects such as this does not just happen by chance. There are always those behind the scenes helping to make it a reality. I would like to thank all those dear to my heart who made this book possible.

First, I would like to thank Holy Spirit for helping me write each devotional to inspire you and add value to your life.

Judith Taylor, my editor, and publisher. You are such a vital part of making my dreams a reality and I would not want to be on this adventure with anyone else. Thank you for doing what you do to make my projects come to life. I appreciate your kindness and your affirmations to ensure everything is just part of the process. Thank you.

Linda Starks, my friend, my sister, my prayer warrior, and my intercessor. Thank you for the countless hours you spend covering my business, my projects, and myself in prayer. You have averted countless enemy attacks in my life, and you are priceless to me. Thank you.

Introduction

Now you understand that I have imparted to you my authority to trample over his kingdom. You will trample upon every demon before you and overcome every power Satan possesses. Absolutely nothing will harm you as you walk in this authority.
Luke 10:19

God created you in His image and He has a wonderful plan for you. This plan includes enforcing Satan's defeat and walking in victory by using your power and authority every day of your life.

Walking in power and authority are not things you strive to achieve; you already possess God's power and authority. As a child of God, you are everything that Jesus is. Since Jesus is raised and seated in the place of victory at the right hand of Father God, far above all powers and principalities, and wickedness in high places, you are also raised and seated with Him. As He is, so are you!

Although you are seated in the place of authority in Christ Jesus, power and authority do not just automatically happen in your life. You must build your faith with the Word of God to receive everything Jesus has already paid the price for you to enjoy while you are here on earth.

If you want to be a victorious champion in Christ, I encourage you to read through the pages of this devotional and linger with Holy Spirit to allow Him to reveal God's heart for you and the love He has for you. Do not rush through the pages.

To build your faith to walk in your power and authority, read each scripture out loud and imagine God is speaking directly to you. Add your name to the verse to make it personal as you read it. Allow Holy Spirit to affirm to you that God created you to live victoriously as you walk in His power and His authority. Let Him teach you how to open your mouth and enforce Satan's defeat with your voice.

Meditate on the scriptures, mull them over in your mind, and answer the questions with new revelations from Father God so you can go to the next level of power and authority.

As you begin your journey through this devotional to build your faith walk in your God-given power and authority so you can walk in victory in every area of your life, the prayer I pray for you is from Ephesians 1:17-23: *I pray that the Father of glory, the God of our Lord Jesus Christ, would impart to you the riches of the Spirit of wisdom and the Spirit of revelation to know him through your deepening intimacy with him.*

I pray that the light of God will illuminate the eyes of your understanding, flooding you with light, until you experience the full revelation of the hope of his calling —that is, the wealth of God's glorious inheritances that he finds in us, his holy ones!

I pray that you will continually experience the immeasurable greatness of God's power made available to you through faith. Then your lives will be an advertisement of this immense power as it works through you! This is the mighty power that was released when God raised Christ from the dead and exalted him to the place of highest honor and supreme authority in the heavenly realm! And now he is exalted as first above every ruler, authority, government, and the realm of power in existence! He is gloriously enthroned over every name that is ever praised, not only in this age but in the age that is coming!

And He alone is the leader and source of everything needed in the church. God has put everything beneath the authority of Jesus Christ and has given Him the highest rank above all others. And now we, His church, are His body on the earth and that which fills him who is being filled by it!

Day 1
Made In God's Image

Then God said, "Let us make human beings in our image, to be like us. They will reign over the fish in the sea, the birds in the sky, the livestock, all the wild animals on the earth, and the small animals that scurry along the ground." Genesis 1:26

My child, We made you in Our image before you were born. You are a three-part being, or man, just as I am a three-part being. I am God the Father, Jesus is God in human form, and Holy Spirit is also God.

You cannot separate Us – We are three in one. We each have a distinctive voice and purpose. You are also a three-part person.

The real you is a spirit, you have a soul, which is your mind, will, and emotions, and you live in a body or earth suit. Regardless of what part of you, or Us, you are referring to, it is just as much you as the other two parts of you. The same is true of Me, Jesus, and Holy Spirit.

Because you are made in Our image, you have power and authority to rule and reign in your domain over all the animals in the sea, the sky, and on earth. You even have power and authority over every plan Satan has for your life.

Prayer – *Father God, Thank You, that I am made in Your image. Father, I ask You in Jesus' Name to give me a deeper revelation of the power and authority I walk in because I am Your child. I ask You to show me how to enforce Satan's defeat in my life so I can walk in victory. I ask You to help me lead others in walking in their power and authority.*

Thoughts to Ponder.

You are made in the image of God the Father, which means you are made like Him. The Word tells you to imitate God. Therefore, you can create what you desire in your life just like God created the world. Ask Holy Spirit to create an image of what you want, then use your faith to paint a picture of it. Once you do this, use your faith-filled words to speak it into existence.

Taking Action To Walk In Authority.

What is one thing from this verse God is affirming to you now?

_____

_____

_____

After meditating on this verse, how does it inspire you to take action to walk in your God-given power and authority?

_____

_____

_____

How will you apply this verse to your prayer life so you can begin walking in your spiritual power and authority to live a life of victory?

_____

_____

_____

Day 2
You Have Binding Power

Receive this truth: Whatever you forbid on earth will be considered to be forbidden in heaven, and whatever you release on earth will be considered to be released in heaven. Matthew 18:18

My precious child, you have the ability to bind the power of Satan in your life and experience days of Heaven on earth. I tell you this truth, if it is not in Heaven, you do not need to permit it to come or stay in your life.

You have been given the power and authority to bring what is in Heaven into your life when you bind the works of Satan and loose my goodness into your life by using your faith-filled words to decree what you desire to manifest in your life.

There is no sickness in Heaven, so you do not need to allow sickness in your body. There is no lack in Heaven so you should not tolerate lack or scarcity in your life. There is no sadness in Heaven so your life can be overflowing with joy.

Use your faith to bind sickness and loose healing into your body and your faith will bring healing to you. Bind lack and loose increased finances, promotion, and debt cancellation and they will come to you. Bind depression and sadness and loose peace and joy to fill you to overflowing.

P rayer – *Father, thank You, for giving me the power to bind Satan's influence and power in my life and loose it from its assignment against me. Thank You that when I bind and loose Satan's power from my life, it is bound and released. When I loose Your power and goodness into my life, I can experience Your power and days of Heaven on earth.*

Thoughts to Ponder.

God has given you power and authority to enforce Satan's defeat in your life every day through the prayer of binding and loosing. You can use Jesus' Name and your faith to bind Satan's influence in your life and loose the Spirit of Truth, which is the Holy Spirit's power, into your life so you can bring about change and enjoy days of Heaven on earth.

Taking Action To Walk In Authority.

What is one thing from this verse God is affirming to you now?
___
___
___

After meditating on this verse, how does it inspire you to take action to walk in your God-given power and authority?
___
___
___

How will you apply this verse to your prayer life so you can begin walking in your spiritual power and authority to live a life of victory?
___
___
___

Day 3
You Have a Spirit of Power

For God will never give you the spirit of fear, but the Holy Spirit who gives you mighty power, love, and self-control. 2 Timothy 1:7

My treasured child, you have nothing to fear because fear is not of Me. You do not need to fear man and what he thinks he can do to you for I am with you. You do not need to fear the winds and waves of the storm because I have given you authority over the winds and waves to tell them 'peace be still.' Just as Jesus spoke to the wind and waves and they obeyed Him, you have that same power and authority.

I gave you that power and authority through My Son, Jesus, and My Holy Spirit. You have more power and authority than you realize. I have given you the power to raise the dead as well as revive the dead things in your life.

I have given you My love; both to enjoy and give away to others. Love covers a multitude of sins, and My desire is that you love yourself and understand you are valuable to me so you can pour My love out onto others.

And last, I have given you a sound mind which includes a spirit of self-control or self-discipline so you can overcome every lie of the enemy in this life. You do have the mind of Christ.

Prayer – *Lord, I resist fear and demand it to go because it is not of You. Thank You for giving me a spirit of power, love, and self-control. I ask You to give me more revelation of the power and authority I have so I can enforce Satan's defeat. Father, I ask You to help me walk in Your power so I can love like You love and share Your love with others.*

Thoughts to Ponder.

You are created in the image of God and have the Holy Spirit living on the inside of you empowering you to walk in His power and authority. Jesus gave you this power and authority when He gave you the keys to the Kingdom. You can release God's power in your life by praying in other tongues, or your Heavenly language, and decreeing and believing God's Word.

Taking Action To Walk In Authority.

What is one thing from this verse God is affirming to you now?

_____
_____
_____

After meditating on this verse, how does it inspire you to take action to walk in your God-given power and authority?

_____
_____
_____

How will you apply this verse to your prayer life so you can begin walking in your spiritual power and authority to live a life of victory?

_____
_____
_____

Day 4
Walking In Your Authority

The crowd was awestruck and kept saying among themselves, "What is this new teaching that comes with such authority? With merely a word he commands demons to come out and they obey him!" Mark 1:27

My beloved child, because you are my child, made in My image, My power and authority reside on the inside of you. You have the ability to do the same mighty acts of power that Jesus did when He walked on the earth and ministered to people.

I told you in My Word that you would do greater works than He did because He was coming back to Heaven and is now seated at My right hand. This is the place of authority and is the symbolization of victory you can refer to for your life. He has finished His assignment.

Now, as My child, you are raised and seated with Jesus in this place of victory, and you have the same authority in which He operated. Therefore, you can speak to demons, and they will obey you just as they obeyed Jesus.

You have the power within you to demolish all the works of Satan in your life, your family's lives, in your area or region, and even in nations. However, you must walk into that authority by opening your mouth and speaking with authority.

I have delegated My authority to you so you can destroy all the demonic forces that are destroying your life or the lives of those you love.

Prayer - *Lord, as your child, I am asking You to help me realize I am created in Your image, and You have already given me power and authority to destroy all the works of Satan and every demonic force that would try to hinder me. Thank You for giving me the authority to enforce Satan's defeat in my life and the lives of those I love.*

Thoughts to Ponder.

As Jesus is, so are you on the earth today. The same power and authority Jesus walked in to enforce Satan's defeat is still available to you right now. It is God's power and authority to annihilate Satan's power in your life. You activate this power and walk in this authority by knowing God's power backs you up when you command Satan to stop.

Taking Action To Walk In Authority.

What is one thing from this verse God is affirming to you now?

_____

_____

_____

After meditating on this verse, how does it inspire you to take action to walk in your God-given power and authority?

_____

_____

_____

How will you apply this verse to your prayer life so you can begin walking in your spiritual power and authority to live a life of victory?

_____

_____

_____

Day 5
You Have All Authority

Then Jesus came close to them and said, "All authority of the universe has been given to me. Now wherever you go, make disciples of all nations...and never forget that I am with you every day, even to the completion of this age." Matthew 28:18-20

My tenacious child, it is time for you to once again step out in your authority to do what I have assigned you to do. Your authority is the same authority that Jesus walked in when He was performing miracles, signs, and wonders during His three years of ministry here on earth.

Jesus told His disciples He was given all the authority of the universe. He was walking in this authority everywhere He went and in everything He did. Demons obeyed His words. The wind and the waves obeyed His voice, and trees obeyed Him.

Jesus is always the same, yesterday, today, and tomorrow. What He told His disciples then, He is telling you today. "Go! I have given you all of My authority and I am with you wherever you go!"

P*rayer - Lord, I thank You, for giving me the ability to walk in the same authority that Jesus walked in while He was here on the earth. Thank You, Jesus, that You are always with me wherever I go. Father, I am determined to walk in my authority to change my world for the better. Wherever You send me I will go.*

Thoughts to Ponder.

Jesus gave His disciples an assignment then told them to "Go!" He reassured them that He was always going to be with them wherever they went. Today, Jesus is telling you the same thing. He is giving you an assignment and telling you to "Go!" You can have the confidence to know that He is always going to be with you to help you fulfill that assignment wherever you go.

Taking Action To Walk In Authority.

What is one thing from this verse God is affirming to you now?

_____

_____

_____

After meditating on this verse, how does it inspire you to take action to walk in your God-given power and authority?

_____

_____

_____

How will you apply this verse to your prayer life so you can begin walking in your spiritual power and authority to live a life of victory?

_____

_____

_____

Day 6
Your Belief Causes Miracles

And these miracle signs will accompany those who believe: They will drive out demons in the power of my name. They will speak in tongues. They will be supernaturally protected from snakes and from drinking anything poisonous. They will lay hands on the sick and heal them. Mark 16:17-18

My audacious child, I have made you to be courageous and full of faith regardless of what you may be feeling with your emotions or seeing with your natural eyes right now in this moment.

I have given you the authority to walk in My power to change your world and the lives of those around you. You must believe that you have My power, and you can operate in it to drive out the enemy and enforce his defeat.

As My child, when you accepted Jesus as your Lord, I immediately filled you with My Spirit. You have the ability to pray and speak in your Heavenly language, or in other tongues, to release My power in your life.

You have My supernatural protection upon you to keep you safe from anything Satan tries to do to harm you. If you inadvertently drink something that may harm you, I will protect you.

I am commanding you to lay hands on the sick and heal them because I have given you the power and the authority to do so. Your faith will produce an action in the natural realm that will activate a chain reaction in the spiritual realm.

Prayer - *Father, Thank You, for increasing my faith to walk in Your power and authority. I believe I will cast out demons in the power of Jesus' name. I will speak in tongues and be supernaturally protected from Satan's schemes. I will lay hands on the sick and heal them.*

Thoughts to Ponder.

Your belief and faith in God's power and authority working in and through you will cause Satan and his enemy forces to take notice. When you realize the power and authority you walk in as God's child, demons tremble when you open your mouth and decree what will happen to Satan and the realms of darkness. You release God's power by praying in the Spirit.

Taking Action To Walk In Authority.

What is one thing from this verse God is affirming to you now?

_____
_____
_____

After meditating on this verse, how does it inspire you to take action to walk in your God-given power and authority?

_____
_____
_____

How will you apply this verse to your prayer life so you can begin walking in your spiritual power and authority to live a life of victory?

_____
_____
_____

Day 7
Jesus Gives You His Authority

Now you understand that I have imparted to you my authority to trample over his kingdom. You will trample upon every demon before you and overcome every power Satan possesses. Absolutely nothing will harm you as you walk in this authority. Luke 10:19

My child, when you realize your name is written in the journals of Heaven and that you belong to My Kingdom, every demon will submit to you as you walk in your authority.

Jesus watched as I kicked Satan out of Heaven. Then He defeated Satan and every demonic force for you, once and for all when He was crucified, rose from the dead, and took His seat in Heaven at My right hand.

Now, your true source of authority comes directly from Jesus. With the authority I have given you through Him, nothing can harm you as you walk in your authority.

However, you must realize you have the same authority Jesus has, and then you must speak My Word and decree My Word to exercise this authority that you have available to you.

As you walk in your authority, every snake and scorpion, which is simply a representation of Satan's demonic powers, that come before you, you have the power to defeat them.

Prayer - *Father, You are Lord Supreme over Heaven and earth! You have hidden the great revelation of Your authority over Satan from those who are proud and those wise in their own eyes. You share this revelation with those who humble themselves before You, so, Father, I humble myself before You and ask for a greater revelation of Your authority and power.*

Thoughts to Ponder.

It pleases God to give hidden revelations of His authority to those who are like trusting children. Challenge yourself today to take God at His Word and make the Bible the final authority in your life. He takes great pleasure in watching you walk in your authority to enforce Satan's defeat and trample over every demonic force in the kingdom of darkness.

Taking Action To Walk In Authority.

What is one thing from this verse God is affirming to you now?

_____
_____
_____

After meditating on this verse, how does it inspire you to take action to walk in your God-given power and authority?

_____
_____
_____

How will you apply this verse to your prayer life so you can begin walking in your spiritual power and authority to live a life of victory?

_____
_____
_____

Day 8
You Have Imparted Authority

Jesus summoned together his twelve apostles and imparted to them authority over every demon and the power to heal every disease. Luke 9:1

My child, you walk in the same authority that the twelve disciples walked in when Jesus called them together and gave them His authority over every demon and the power to heal the sick

Authority is delegated power. When someone delegates their authority to you, the value of that authority is determined by the power that is backing up that authority.

In the natural realm, policemen have delegated authority from their police chief, who has authority given to him by the mayor.

When Jesus delegates His authority to you, I am the power that is backing you up. Satan and every demon are obligated to acknowledge your authority.

You are not operating in your own authority when you speak to demonic forces and heal the sick of every disease. You are functioning under the authority of the Kingdom of Heaven and all of My power is backing you up.

You have My authority to speak to demons and Satan himself and tell them to leave you alone and stop hindering you. They will obey You.

Prayer – *Father God, thank You, for giving me Your authority, or Your delegated power, to enforce Satan's defeat and heal the sick of every disease. I recognize that Your power is behind me to enforce what I speak. Starting today I am strong in Your power, and I exercise my authority over Satan and his demonic forces to enforce their defeat in my life.*

Thoughts to Ponder.

As a child of God who walks in your authority, you can be reassured that when you speak to Satan and his demons, all of the power of God's Kingdom is backing you up to enforce Satan's defeat. Because of your covenant with Jesus, this power belongs to you. He paid the price with His precious Blood so you can enforce Satan's defeat and walk in victory.

Taking Action To Walk In Authority.

What is one thing from this verse God is affirming to you now?
_____
_____
_____

After meditating on this verse, how does it inspire you to take action to walk in your God-given power and authority?
_____
_____
_____

How will you apply this verse to your prayer life so you can begin walking in your spiritual power and authority to live a life of victory?
_____
_____
_____

Day 9
Your Glorious Inheritance

Your hearts can soar with joyful gratitude when you think of how God made you worthy to receive the glorious inheritance freely given to us by living in the light. He has rescued us completely from the tyrannical rule of darkness and has translated us into the kingdom realm of his beloved Son. Colossians 1:12-13

You are My precious child, and I made you worthy to receive all the blessings, all the power, and all the authority that Jesus shed His Blood for you to walk in freedom and victory. Today, I ask you to think about the inheritance that I have given you. This day is your day to celebrate with great joy that you no longer live in Satan's domain of the realm of darkness. You are no longer Satan's puppet. He cannot rule over you like he once did before you chose to come out of the realm of darkness and live in the light of My Kingdom.

I rescued you and made you gloriously free when you accepted My Son, Jesus, as your Savior. He made you free. You became a brand-new person, one that never existed before. Now, you cannot only do everything Jesus did when He walked on the earth, but you can do even greater works since He came back to Heaven with Me.

You can have everything Jesus has. He delegated all of His power and authority to you so you can walk in victory and that is the reason your heart can celebrate with great joy!

Prayer – *Father, thank You, for delivering me from the realms of darkness and Satan's power. Thank You for my glorious inheritance when I accepted Jesus as my Savior. I am so grateful I now live in Your Kingdom. Thank You for making me worthy to receive my inheritance. I am asking for a greater revelation of the power and authority I have available to me.*

Thoughts to Ponder.

You have a glorious inheritance waiting for you to partake of. All the power of the Kingdom of Heaven is available to you and backing you up as you walk in your God-given authority to bring God's light into the kingdom of darkness. Boldly decree God's Word with confidence and authority and you will not only change your atmosphere, you will change your world.

Taking Action To Walk In Authority.

What is one thing from this verse God is affirming to you now?

_____

_____

_____

After meditating on this verse, how does it inspire you to take action to walk in your God-given power and authority?

_____

_____

_____

How will you apply this verse to your prayer life so you can begin walking in your spiritual power and authority to live a life of victory?

_____

_____

_____

Day 10
You Are Forever Alive

For we have been buried with him into his death. Our "baptism into death" also means we were raised with him when we believed in God's resurrection power, the power that raised him from death's realm. This "realm of death" describes our former state, for we were held in sin's grasp. But now, we've been resurrected out of that "realm of death" never to return, for we are forever alive and forgiven of all our sins! Colossians 2:12-13

My dear child, I would ask you to stop and realize that you have been snatched from the realms of death and darkness when you asked My Son, Jesus, to be your Lord and Savior. You were translated into My glorious Kingdom of Light when you believed Jesus rose from the dead and He is now alive and sitting at My right hand, the place of authority and victory.

You are raised and seated with Him and you will never return to the realm of darkness because you chose Jesus. All your sins are forgiven and will spend eternity with us.

Just as Jesus was buried and defeated death, hell and the grave then He was resurrected and rose victorious, this is your example of how you can and should live your life.

As my child you are full of resurrection power. You are now seated with Jesus far above all demonic power and you have the authority to raise the dead, heal the sick, and walk in victory.

Prayer – *Father, thank You, that all of my sins are forgiven, and I am redeemed from the realms of death and darkness into Your glorious Kingdom of Light. Thank You that I now have resurrection power living on the inside of me because I made Jesus my Lord. I ask You to give me the boldness to walk in this power and authority shedding light into the darkness.*

Thoughts to Ponder.

Your completeness and God's hidden treasures or spiritual wealth are found in the person of Jesus Christ. These endless riches of revelation knowledge are waiting for you to discover them. Just as you used your faith to receive Jesus as your Savior, use your faith to walk in everything Jesus accomplished for you now that you are resurrected out of the realm of death.

Taking Action To Walk In Authority.

What is one thing from this verse God is affirming to you now?

_____

_____

_____

After meditating on this verse, how does it inspire you to take action to walk in your God-given power and authority?

_____

_____

_____

How will you apply this verse to your prayer life so you can begin walking in your spiritual power and authority to live a life of victory?

_____

_____

_____

Day 11
Heirs of God Himself

And since we are his true children, we qualify to share all his treasures, for indeed, we are heirs of God himself. And since we are joined to Christ, we also inherit all that he is and all that he has. We will experience being co-glorified with him provided that we accept his sufferings as our own. Romans 8:17

Before you knew Me, I knew you. I created you and designed you to have a relationship with Me. My sweet child, when you accepted My Son, Jesus, as your Savior, you became My most precious child.

You are truly my child, and you qualify to share in all of the treasures that Jesus has. You are my heir and that entitles you to take ownership of everything that Jesus had when He lived on the earth and now that He has rose again and is seated in Heaven with Me.

You are no longer My servant, you are My son, my daughter and I see you through the Blood of Jesus. This means that I do not see male or female, I simply see you as if I am seeing My Son, Jesus.

As My Son, Jesus was a man operating in My Anointing doing signs, wonders, and miracles. You can do these works and ever greater works because you have My Holy Spirit with you. You can even walk in the same authority and power that Jesus walked in as you go about living your everyday life. I will use you to bring My Glory into the earth today.

Prayer – *Father God, I ask You to give me greater revelation of the fact that as Your child, as Your heir, I have access to all of Your treasures. I have the same treasures that Jesus has. I am asking You to give me knowledge and wisdom as to how to walk in the same authority and power that Jesus walked in while He was here on the earth.*

Thoughts to Ponder.

You became a joint heir with Jesus Christ when you accepted Him as your Savior. This is truly one of the most amazing phenomenon in the Bible; the miracle of making you brand new, as if you never existed before. Then God gave you the very same authority and power that Jesus used during His three years of ministry here on the earth.

Taking Action To Walk In Authority.

What is one thing from this verse God is affirming to you now?

_____

_____

_____

After meditating on this verse, how does it inspire you to take action to walk in your God-given power and authority?

_____

_____

_____

How will you apply this verse to your prayer life so you can begin walking in your spiritual power and authority to live a life of victory?

_____

_____

_____

Day 12
Stand Up To The Devil

So then, surrender to God. Stand up to the devil and resist him and he will flee in agony. James 4:7

The world has nothing to offer you that can compare to My love and the glorious wonders of My Kingdom, My dear child. The world has countless temptations that appear to bring you satisfaction; however, they only offer temporary fulfillment.

I have called you out of the world into my marvelous light so I can have an intimate relationship with you. This relationship will satisfy you completely and you will not have a desire for the things of this world.

As you surrender to My love and My plans for your life, it becomes easier to resist Satan's plans for your life. His plan is to draw you into the world's way of thinking and doing things. When you take on the world's ways, you are flirting with the world's values, and this places you at odds with Me.

If you choose to be friends with the world, you make yourself an enemy to Me. When My Spirit breathed life into you, His purpose was to have more and more of you because He is a jealous Lover.

Although it is not always easy, I am asking you to resist Satan's pull on your life and surrender to Me. I will give you grace and empower you to resist him so he will flee in agony.

Prayer – *Father, thank You, for loving me and drawing me out of this world's system into Your Kingdom of Light through Your Holy Spirit. I am so grateful that You have given me authority to resist Satan and trample on him and his demonic forces. I ask You to open my eyes and expose the enemy's tactics against my life so I can stand firm and resist him.*

Thoughts to Ponder.

The Holy Spirit always pursues you relentlessly and draws you close to God because He longs to have an intimate relationship with you. He takes it very personally when you turn away from Him to pursue a friendship with the world. You must choose to walk in your authority and resist Satan by standing up to him. He will flee because of the One who is standing with you.

Taking Action To Walk In Authority.

What is one thing from this verse God is affirming to you now?

_____
_____
_____

After meditating on this verse, how does it inspire you to take action to walk in your God-given power and authority?

_____
_____
_____

How will you apply this verse to your prayer life so you can begin walking in your spiritual power and authority to live a life of victory?

_____
_____
_____

Day 13
You Have Spiritual Blessings

Every spiritual blessing in the heavenly realm has already been lavished upon us as a love gift from our wonderful heavenly Father, the Father of our Lord Jesus—all because he sees us wrapped into Christ. This is why we celebrate him with all our hearts! Ephesians 1:3

My child, I love you beyond measure. Because I see you and Jesus as one, My love for Him is the same love I have for you. The same love and spiritual giftings I gave Him, I am giving to you. I have given you many blessings in the physical realm. However, the greatest blessings that I give you are the spiritual blessings that are a benefit of your relationship with Me through My Son, Jesus.

The blessings I have given you include the gift of being extended My grace and Me offering you the greatest gift of all time which is salvation through My Son. By believing in My Son, I chose to make you holy and blameless before Me. Now you have full access to Me and can come to Me as My child.

The blood Jesus shed for you has taken away the guilt of your sins so you can stand before Me, forgiven and perfectly accepted, redeemed from Satan's plan for your life.

When you align yourself with Me by using your faith, you become part of My perfect plan and purpose for your life. A plan that gives you My power and authority to live a life of victory regardless of the challenges you may face.

Prayer - *Thank You, Father, for revealing the many spiritual blessings You have given to me. Blessings that I have taken for granted many times. Thank You for sending Your Son, Jesus, to pay the price for me to have a relationship with You and be Your child. I ask You to help me be more aware of the spiritual blessings You have given me so I can walk in my authority.*

Thoughts to Ponder.

To enjoy all of God's spiritual blessings, it begins by accepting Jesus as your Savior and then having a personal relationship with Him. Your salvation opens the door to the blessings of being called God's son, being redeemed, justified, sanctified. You are given an inheritance that includes all the riches of glory, God's presence, and an eternal home with Him.

Taking Action To Walk In Authority.

What is one thing from this verse God is affirming to you now?

_____
_____
_____

After meditating on this verse, how does it inspire you to take action to walk in your God-given power and authority?

_____
_____
_____

How will you apply this verse to your prayer life so you can begin walking in your spiritual power and authority to live a life of victory?

_____
_____
_____

Day 14
Stand Victorious In His Power

Now my beloved ones, I have saved these most important truths for last: Be supernaturally infused with strength through your life union with the Lord Jesus. Stand victorious with the force of his explosive power flowing in and through you. Ephesians 6:10

My precious child, are you weary from your daily routine and the hustle and bustle of your life? I encourage you to come away with me. Stop what you are doing. It will be there when you come back to it.

Make time for Me. Come away My beloved and let Me infuse you with My power and My strength, so you can do what you need to do with ease. My Spirit is living inside you to help you, and He will strengthen you when you think you cannot go another step.

It may seem awkward at first, but the more you spend time praying in your first language, your Heavenly language, you will sense My Holy Spirit's power surging through you. You will sense His power strengthening you to keep going and live a victorious life.

You can tap into My power every minute of every day to be strengthened supernaturally. I encourage you to keep your mind focused on Jesus and the price He paid for you to walk in power and victory. All the benefits Jesus enjoys are yours to enjoy as well. As Jesus is, so are you in this world.

Prayer – *Father God, thank You, for infusing me with Your supernatural power and strength because I am living my life united with Your Son, Jesus. I decree I am standing victorious every day with the force of Holy Spirit's explosive power flowing in and through me.*

Thoughts to Ponder.

Why would you want to live life in your strength when God has made supernatural power and strength available to you through His Son, Jesus? Jesus gave you His authority and His power to enforce Satan's defeat every day when you wake up! The Holy Spirit lives inside you and infuses you with His strength to walk in victory.

Taking Action To Walk In Authority.

What is one thing from this verse God is affirming to you now?
_____
_____
_____

After meditating on this verse, how does it inspire you to take action to walk in your God-given power and authority?
_____
_____
_____

How will you apply this verse to your prayer life so you can begin walking in your spiritual power and authority to live a life of victory?
_____
_____
_____

Day 15
You Are Destined For Victory

Because of this, you must wear all the armor that God provides so you're protected as you confront the slanderer, for you are destined for all things and will rise victorious. Ephesians 6:13

    I created you to be My victorious warrior, dear child and have equipped you for spiritual battle. You are not weak or defenseless against the enemy's tactics.

    As you rise from your sleep each day, put on My complete set of armor that I have provided for you so you will be protected as you fight against the evil strategies of your accuser who is Satan, and his demonic forces!

    You know your hand-to-hand combat is not with human beings, but with the highest principalities and authorities operating in rebellion under the heavenly realms, here on earth.

    These demon-gods and evil spirits do have the power to hold this dark world in bondage. However, they are not more powerful than you. This is why I tell you that you must wear all the armor that I provide for you, so you are protected as you confront your accuser.

    You are destined and equipped to conquer the enemy and all the things he tries to bring into your life because I created you to stand in victory. I assure you that you will rise victorious over the enemy's ploys.

Prayer – *Father God, thank You, for equipping me beforehand for the spiritual battle against Satan and His demonic forces. I realize You have created me to win; however, I am asking You, in the Name of Jesus, to give me more revelation and a clearer understanding of the power and authority I walk in because I am Your child.*

Thoughts to Ponder.

When you made Jesus your Lord and Savior, God gave you power and authority over Satan and all his demonic forces and wickedness in high places. As you put on the complete armor of God you are protected against the enemy's attacks. God equipped you for battle, and He destined you to always win when you have a challenge or negative situation facing you.

Taking Action To Walk In Authority.

What is one thing from this verse God is affirming to you now?
_____
_____
_____

After meditating on this verse, how does it inspire you to take action to walk in your God-given power and authority?
_____
_____
_____

How will you apply this verse to your prayer life so you can begin walking in your spiritual power and authority to live a life of victory?
_____
_____
_____

Day 16
Be Strong And Courageous

Have I not commanded you? Be strong and courageous. Do not be frightened, and do not be dismayed, for the Lord your God is with you wherever you go. Joshua 1:9

You are my cherished child whom I take great delight in. The things I am asking you to do are within your ability to do them. They may seem beyond your capabilities at the moment; however, I have already given you the power to accomplish them.

I recognize thoughts of self-doubt, disbelief, and skepticism. Take these thoughts captive and rise up; get up full of confidence and power!

Now is the time to actually believe all things are possible for you and you can achieve the prize. Pull up your courage and take your place of authority today. Step out in faith and do it! I have told you to do this thing, to possess your land, to fulfill your dream. Take action!

I am with you! Every place your feet trod shall be yours. No man will be able to stop what I have planned for you. Be strong and courageous because I am with you. I will not leave you, fail you or forsake you. You can do it!

Prayer – *Father, I am asking You to give me the courage and the boldness to get up and step out to do what You have assigned me to do. Thank You for equipping me to answer the call and the assignment You created for me. I decree that I am taking every negative thought captive to the will of God, and I will possess the land You have prepared for me.*

Thoughts to Ponder.

God tells you to only be strong and of good courage, at least three times in the first chapter of Joshua. He says to not be frightened or dismayed because He is with you wherever you go. He is not going to tell you to do something you are not capable of doing. Your obedience will cause future generations to receive the inheritance Father God has prepared for them.

Taking Action To Walk In Authority.

What is one thing from this verse God is affirming to you now?

_____
_____
_____

After meditating on this verse, how does it inspire you to take action to walk in your God-given power and authority?

_____
_____
_____

How will you apply this verse to your prayer life so you can begin walking in your spiritual power and authority to live a life of victory?

_____
_____
_____

Day 17
Satan Is Stripped Of Authority

Then Jesus made a public spectacle of all the powers and principalities of darkness, stripping away from them every weapon and all their spiritual authority and power to accuse us. And by the power of the cross, Jesus led them around as prisoners in a procession of triumph. He was not their prisoner; they were his!
Colossians 2:15

Because you are My child, you are redeemed from the curse of the enemy's stronghold in your life. You are entitled to all of the benefits Jesus paid the price for you to walk in. When Jesus went to the cross and took your place, He paid your ransom to get you back from the enemy. Then He gave you His power and authority to enforce Satan's defeat in your life.

Jesus canceled out every legal violation you had on your record prior to becoming My child. He erased all your sins and the old nature of Adam, then Jesus gave you His nature. You are set free of every trace of sin by the power of the Blood of Jesus, and they cannot be retrieved.

Jesus made a public spectacle of all the principalities and powers of darkness while He was in hell. He stripped away every weapon from Satan and his demonic forces and all their spiritual authority and power to accuse you. Then Jesus led them through hell in a celebration parade making an open show of them for all to see they were defeated.

Prayer – *Father, Thank You, for sending Your Son, Jesus, to pay the price for me to walk in total victory over Satan and his demonic forces. I am encouraged and strengthened in every way as I plant my spiritual roots into the life of Jesus. He is my Lord, and I am devoted to Him. Thank You for establishing me and infusing me with Your power.*

Thoughts to Ponder.

Jesus spoiled all Satan's powers when He died on the cross. He was in the spirit-realm between the day He was crucified and the day He was resurrected. He destroyed death, the powers of darkness, and every evil work of the enemy through His shed Blood on the cross. He stripped Satan of all his weapons. You now have the authority to enforce Satan's defeat in your life.

Taking Action To Walk In Authority.

What is one thing from this verse God is affirming to you now?
_____
_____
_____

After meditating on this verse, how does it inspire you to take action to walk in your God-given power and authority?
_____
_____
_____

How will you apply this verse to your prayer life so you can begin walking in your spiritual power and authority to live a life of victory?
_____
_____
_____

Day 18
I Have God's Resurrection Power

And I continually long to know the wonders of Jesus and to experience the overflowing power of his resurrection working in me. I will be one with him in his sufferings and become like him in his death. Only then will I be able to experience complete oneness with him in his resurrection from the realm of death. Philippians 3:10-11

My desire for you, My sweet child, is to see your passion be consumed with Jesus and that you are no longer clinging to your own righteousness by trying to keep the Letter of the Law.

Because you are My child, your righteousness is now based on the faithfulness of Jesus which is the very righteousness that comes from Me.

I long for you to continually know the wonders of Jesus and to experience the overflowing power of His resurrection working in you. To do this, realize that when Jesus died, you died with Him. When He was resurrected, you were resurrected with Him.

You can experience the complete oneness with Him in His resurrection from the realm of death as you live your life here on earth.

Prayer – *Father, I am asking You, in the Name of Jesus, to give me a desire for a greater revelation and a better understanding to know the wonderful miracle-working power of Jesus. I want to experience the overflowing power of His resurrection working in me. My request is that I will realize this power.*

Thoughts to Ponder.

When Jesus said yes to God, He said yes to you. Yes, to freedom. Yes, to redemption. Yes, to your sanctification and your righteousness. Your righteousness is not your self-righteousness. Rather, Jesus' faithfulness to say yes, became your righteousness from God. The power you walk in today is the same resurrection power that raised Jesus from the dead.

Taking Action To Walk In Authority.

What is one thing from this verse God is affirming to you now?
___
___
___

After meditating on this verse, how does it inspire you to take action to walk in your God-given power and authority?
___
___
___

How will you apply this verse to your prayer life so you can begin walking in your spiritual power and authority to live a life of victory?
___
___
___

Day 19
Your Mighty Spiritual Weapons

For although we live in the natural realm, we don't wage a military campaign employing human weapons, using manipulation to achieve our aims. Instead, our spiritual weapons are energized with divine power to effectively dismantle the defenses behind which people hide. We can demolish every deceptive fantasy that opposes God and break through every arrogant attitude that is raised up in defiance of the true knowledge of God. We capture, like prisoners of war, every thought and insist that it bow in obedience to the Anointed One. 2 Corinthians 10:3-5

    My child, I do not want you to mistakenly believe that you are living by the standards of this physical world. I would rather you believe the truth that you are living by Holy Spirit's wisdom and power. Although you walk in the flesh and live in this natural realm, you do not carry-on spiritual warfare according to the flesh of using manipulation to achieve your goals.

    You have authority to demolish all deceptive arguments opposing God, breaking through every arrogant attitude that rises in defiance of the true knowledge of God. You can capture every thought or scheme defying the authority of God, and demand it bow in obedience to God.

Prayer– *Thank You, Father, for giving me the revelation that although I live in this natural world, I do not wage war against Satan using natural weapons. I ask You to give me a greater revelation of the spiritual authority I walk in and the spiritual weapons I have available to me to enforce Satan's defeat so I can pull every thought captive to Your will.*

Thoughts to Ponder.

You have the authority to destroy every deceptive argument or proud thing that raises itself against God. You have the power to break every arrogant attitude that rises in defiance of the genuine understanding of God. You are armed with dynamic weaponry to capture every thought that defies the authority of God and insist that it **give up and obey Christ.**

Taking Action To Walk In Authority.

What is one thing from this verse God is affirming to you now?

_____
_____
_____

After meditating on this verse, how does it inspire you to take action to walk in your God-given power and authority?

_____
_____
_____

How will you apply this verse to your prayer life so you can begin walking in your spiritual power and authority to live a life of victory?

_____
_____
_____

Day 20
Your Miracle-Working Power

I tell you this timeless truth: The person who follows me in faith, believing in me, will do the same mighty miracles that I do—even greater miracles than these because I go to be with my Father! John 14:12

My cherished child, I have told you before and I want to tell you again, I love you so dearly. Thank you for following My Son, Jesus, and believing in His miracle-working power since you became My child. Your faith is a priceless weapon to Me.

Just as I was with Jesus, I am with you today! He only spoke the words He heard Me say and He only did the work I told Him to do. This is your example of how I will work through you.

My Holy Spirit lives in you and He is doing a mighty work in you. Not only is He doing a mighty work in you, He is also doing mighty works through you. Miracles, signs, and wonders will follow you because you believe in My Son.

You will stand in amazement at the things I will do through you as you surrender your will to My will and believe all things are possible for you to accomplish. You can believe all things are possible because the resurrection power that raised Jesus from the dead, is the same resurrection power that lives on the inside of you empowering you to do the works I have called you to do.

Prayer - *Thank You, Father God, for Your Son, Jesus. I ask You to give me a greater revelation of the authority I have and the power that is contained in my faith. I believe in Your Son, Jesus, and am asking You to give me opportunities to do greater miracles than He did because He arose from the dead and is now seated at your right hand.*

Thoughts to Ponder.

When you read through the Gospels – Matthew, Mark, Luke, and John – you read about the miracles Jesus performed during His three years of ministry here on the earth and how He only said what He heard His Father say. He only did what His Father told Him to do. You have the ability and resurrection power inside of you to do the same things Jesus did, and even greater works than He did.

Taking Action To Walk In Authority.

What is one thing from this verse God is affirming to you now?
_____
_____
_____

After meditating on this verse, how does it inspire you to take action to walk in your God-given power and authority?
_____
_____
_____

How will you apply this verse to your prayer life so you can begin walking in your spiritual power and authority to live a life of victory?
_____
_____
_____

Day 21

Remain Alert – Stand Strong

Be well balanced and always alert, because your enemy the devil, roams around incessantly, like a roaring lion looking for its prey to devour. Take a decisive stand against him and resist his every attack with strong, vigorous faith. For you know that your believing brothers and sisters around the world are experiencing the same kinds of troubles you endure. 1 Peter 5:8-9

My precious child, do not allow the cares of life to press in on you or overwhelm you. I want to encourage you to pour out all of your worries and stress upon Jesus and leave them there because He is always tenderly caring for you.

Jesus is watching over you so take every care and anxiety and give them to Him. Your enemy is Satan, and he roams around continually, like a roaring lion looking for prey to devour so remain stable and alert.

If you do not bring all your worries, anxieties, and cares to Jesus, Satan will use disappointment, discouragement, and depression to devour you.

Just as a lion goes after young, weak, and straggling prey, Satan goes after the person that is isolated, alone, discouraged, and depressed to devour them.

Now is the time to take a decisive stand against Satan and resist every attack with your strong faith.

Prayer – *Father, thank You, that Jesus is always watching over me because He cares for me. As an act of my faith, I am placing all of my cares, fears, anxieties, and concerns onto Jesus so Satan cannot isolate and discourage me. I am asking You to give me the strength to resist Satan and his plan to devour me through disappointment and depression.*

Thoughts to Ponder.

Satan's plan for you is to use disappointments in your life to discourage you. He wants to separate you from your community of friends, so you feel alone, discouraged, and depressed. Then he can devour and destroy you. Instead of focusing on the disappointment, go to Jesus and give Him your cares. Resist the temptation to handle things by yourself.

Taking Action To Walk In Authority.

What is one thing from this verse God is affirming to you now?

_____

_____

_____

After meditating on this verse, how does it inspire you to take action to walk in your God-given power and authority?

_____

_____

_____

How will you apply this verse to your prayer life so you can begin walking in your spiritual power and authority to live a life of victory?

_____

_____

_____

Day 22
You Reign As A King

Death once held us in its grip, and by the blunder of one man, death reigned as king over humanity. But now, how much more are we held in the grip of grace and continue reigning as kings in life, enjoying our regal freedom through the gift of perfect righteousness in the one and only Jesus, the Messiah! Romans 5:17

My child, you can have the confidence to know that I will always hold you in the grip of My grace. Although Adam's choice to do what I told him not to do brought spiritual as well as physical death to humanity, My Son, Jesus, has made a way for you to reign in this life.

The choices both Adam and Jesus made affected the whole world. Death passes to all who are in Adam – those who do not accept My Son as their savior – and life passes to all those who choose My Son, Jesus, to be their Lord.

In other words, condemnation came upon every person through one transgression made by Adam. By one righteous act of the sacrifice that Jesus made, all of humanity is made perfectly right with God which leads to a victorious life. This choice is now available to everyone.

Sweet child, because I sent My Son to be the sacrifice in your place, and you chose Him, you can reign as a king in your life. Enjoy your regal freedom through the gift of covenant membership in the one and only Jesus, the Messiah

Prayer – *Father, Thank You, for sending Your Son, Jesus, to put me in right standing with You. I choose Jesus to be my Lord and I know that I am made righteous through His Blood sacrifice. I am asking You to give me a greater revelation of the blessings and privileges I have to rule as a king in my life because of the covenant I have with You.*

Thoughts to Ponder.

You are made righteous, in right standing with God, through the sacrifice Jesus made when He went to the cross and shed His Blood for you. Because of His sacrifice, you now have the authority and power to rule as a king in your life. You are an ambassador of the Kingdom of Heaven and are entitled to everything that Jesus shed His Blood for you to enjoy.

Taking Action To Walk In Authority.

What is one thing from this verse God is affirming to you now?
_____
_____
_____

After meditating on this verse, how does it inspire you to take action to walk in your God-given power and authority?
_____
_____
_____

How will you apply this verse to your prayer life so you can begin walking in your spiritual power and authority to live a life of victory?
_____
_____
_____

Day 23

God's Power Flows Through Faith

I pray that you will continually experience the immeasurable greatness of God's power made available to you through faith. Then your lives will be an advertisement of this immense power as it works through you! This is the mighty power that was released when God raised Christ from the dead and exalted him to the place of highest honor and supreme authority in the heavenly realm! Ephesians 1:19-20

My beloved child, my desire for you is that you would constantly experience the greatness of My power by always using your faith to receive the desires of your heart. As you do this, I will bless you beyond measure and use you as an example of My goodness on the earth so others will have hope.

The power I desire you to experience firsthand is the same resurrection power that was displayed when My Holy Spirit raised Jesus from the dead and then seated Him at My right hand. This is the highest place of honor and authority.

Because you are a joint heir with Jesus, you are entitled to the same benefits that Jesus has. When I raised and exalted Jesus to My right hand, I made His enemies His footstool. Now as My child, I want you to use your faith to realize you are seated with Jesus in the place of authority. I have given you the same power to make your enemies your footstool.

Prayer – *Father God, I ask You to help me continually experience the immeasurable greatness of Your power that is available to me through my faith. Thank You, for using my life as an advertisement of Your immense power working through me! I am asking for a greater revelation of the power that is released when I use my faith to receive Your promises.*

Thoughts to Ponder.

When you made Jesus your Lord, you were automatically raised and seated with Jesus at the right hand of God. You are seated in the place of power and authority over all your enemies. It is God's desire for you to use your power to enforce Satan's defeat and walk in victory. He desires to use you as an example of His goodness and power on the earth because you use faith.

Taking Action To Walk In Authority.

What is one thing from this verse God is affirming to you now?

_____

_____

_____

After meditating on this verse, how does it inspire you to take action to walk in your God-given power and authority?

_____

_____

_____

How will you apply this verse to your prayer life so you can begin walking in your spiritual power and authority to live a life of victory?

_____

_____

_____

Day 24
Your Authority Is In Jesus

And he alone is the leader and source of everything needed in the church. God has put everything beneath the authority of Jesus Christ and has given him the highest rank above all others. And now we, his church, are his body on the earth and that which fills him who is being filled by it! Ephesians 1:22-23

You are My child and I created you to have a relationship with Me through My son, Jesus. Through My Holy Spirit's power, I raised Jesus from the dead and seated Him at My right hand in the highest place of rank, power, and authority above all others.

My design for the church is for Jesus to be the leader and source of everything the church needs. On the earth, Jesus is the head of the church, and you are His body because you are His church.

The church is not peripheral to the world; rather the world is peripheral to the church. The church is where Jesus speaks, acts, and fills everything with His presence.

My desire for you, sweet child, is that you be filled to overflowing with the full measure of My presence. When you are flooded with My presence, you are completely empowered to fulfill My purpose for your life.

Prayer – *Father, I come boldly into the Throne Room of Grace to ask You to open the eyes of my understanding so I may know the greatness of Your power working in my life. I am humbling myself before You and am asking You to give me spiritual wisdom and understanding and fill me to overflowing with Your presence so I may fulfill Your call on my life.*

Thoughts to Ponder.

Jesus is seated in the place of authority above every ruler, government, and the realm of power. He alone is the leader and source of everything the church needs. God has put everything beneath the authority of Jesus. He has conquered, subdued, and now rules over all His enemies. As God's child, you are seated with Jesus and have the same power He has.

Taking Action To Walk In Authority.

What is one thing from this verse God is affirming to you now?
_____
_____
_____

After meditating on this verse, how does it inspire you to take action to walk in your God-given power and authority?
_____
_____
_____

How will you apply this verse to your prayer life so you can begin walking in your spiritual power and authority to live a life of victory?
_____
_____
_____

Day 25
Raised And Seated With Jesus

Even when we were dead and doomed in our many sins, he united us into the very life of Christ and saved us by his wonderful grace! He raised us up with Christ the exalted One, and we ascended with him into the glorious perfection and authority of the heavenly realm, for we are now co-seated as one with Christ! Ephesians 2:5-6

Before you became My child, you were dead in your sins and offenses. You lived in the religion, customs, and values of this world. You obeyed Satan who is the dark ruler of the earthly realm and fills the atmosphere with his authority. He works diligently in the hearts of those who are disobedient to the truth of God.

You lived in this dark realm by whatever natural cravings and thoughts your mind dictated to you. This caused you to live as a rebellious child. **Before you chose Me,** I loved you with such great love and showed you My compassion and mercy. However, now that you are My child, you are filled with all of My goodness and power.

When you were dead and living a life of despair, I united you into the very life of Jesus, My anointed Son, and saved you by His wonderful grace! I raised you up with Jesus, and you ascended with Him into the glorious perfection and authority of the heavenly realm. You are now seated as one with Jesus!

Prayer – *Father God, thank You, for drawing me out of this dark world and the rule of Satan by Your grace. I rejoice that I am united with Jesus. I ask You to give me greater revelation of the truth that I am perfect in Jesus. Help me understand that You have already given me authority and power over Satan to enforce his defeat because I am seated at Your right hand.*

Thoughts to Ponder.

God drew you to Himself by His Holy Spirit. It is His grace that saved you. Your 'yes' to God positioned you in the place of victory which is at God's right hand. You are seated in the place of authority with Jesus. Since you are raised and seated with Jesus far above all powers and principalities, you have authority to speak to circumstances and change them.

Taking Action To Walk In Authority.

What is one thing from this verse God is affirming to you now?

_____
_____
_____

After meditating on this verse, how does it inspire you to take action to walk in your God-given power and authority?

_____
_____
_____

How will you apply this verse to your prayer life so you can begin walking in your spiritual power and authority to live a life of victory?

_____
_____
_____

Day 26
God Has Given You Authority

But now, to convince you that the Son of Man has been given authority to forgive sins, I say to this man, 'Stand up, pick up your mat, and walk home.' Immediately the man sprang to his feet and left for home. When the crowds witnessed this miracle, they were awestruck. They shouted praises to God because he had given such authority to human beings. Matthew 9:6-8

My child, I adore you beyond measure. You are a joy to My heart just because you exist. I have so many things I want to share with you. I want you to gain a greater understanding and have more revelation of the limitless power and authority you currently possess and have available to you on an ongoing basis.

The thoughts you are thinking regarding circumstances you and your loved ones are facing today need to be addressed the same way Jesus spoke to situations.

Your older brother, Jesus, paid the price for you to be complete and walk in the fullness of His authority and power. He was not only My Son, but He was also the son of man and I anointed Him to do mighty works on the earth. Just as I have anointed you to do the same.

Now, you can accomplish the easy things as well as the hard things; both healing and forgiveness can flow from you because you are My child. I encourage you to shout My praises because I have given you authority to do these mighty works.

Prayer – *Father, thank You, for anointing me with Your power and authority to speak to the easy as well as the hard situations that I am facing today. I am asking You to give me greater understanding and more revelation knowledge of the limitless power and authority I possess and have available to me on a regular, ongoing basis.*

Thoughts to Ponder.

As God's child, you should rejoice and shout for joy that He has given you limitless power and authority to speak to your situations and command them to change. You have the same authority Jesus has to speak to demonic forces. You can bind Satan and the demons that are tormenting you and loose them from their assignment against you and they will obey you.

Taking Action To Walk In Authority.

What is one thing from this verse God is affirming to you now?
_____
_____
_____

After meditating on this verse, how does it inspire you to take action to walk in your God-given power and authority?
_____
_____
_____

How will you apply this verse to your prayer life so you can begin walking in your spiritual power and authority to live a life of victory?
_____
_____
_____

Day 27
Use Your Power, Not Just Words

For the kingdom realm of God comes with power, not simply impressive words. 1 Corinthians 4:20

My child, when you heard the Good News of the Gospel and stepped into My Kingdom by accepting My Son, Jesus, as your Lord and Savior, I empowered you to do the same works and now, even greater works than Jesus did when He fulfilled His three years of earthly ministry. I encourage you, as My child, to follow the example that Jesus lived before you in the Gospels of Matthew, Mark, Luke, and John. You can also follow the example of Timothy.

Timothy was faithful to Me and dependable to do what He was instructed to do. You can conduct yourself and your life as one who lives in union with Jesus Christ, who is the Anointed One. I ask you to not exalt yourself in the works you are doing on My behalf as you have seen others do.

When you trust Me and tap into My Kingdom realm, it comes with unlimited power, not simply impressive words. You can have the confidence to know that when you humble yourself before Me and ask Me to help you share My Word with people, you are not simply using persuasive words of wisdom; you can expect a demonstration of the Holy Spirit's power to change lives.

Prayer - *Thank You, God, for giving me unlimited access to Your Kingdom power. I humble myself before You today and ask You to fill my mouth with Your Words. Use my hands to do Your miracles here on the earth. I ask You to give me greater revelations of the power that I can operate in because I am Your child. I will always give You the Glory for the works I do.*

Thoughts to Ponder.

God resists the proud person and gives grace to those that humble themselves before Him. If you want to see miracles, signs, and wonders follow you because you believe, always give God the glory for what He does through you. There is nothing that you will not be able to accomplish when you tap into the power of the Kingdom of Heaven.

Taking Action To Walk In Authority.

What is one thing from this verse God is affirming to you now?

_____
_____
_____

After meditating on this verse, how does it inspire you to take action to walk in your God-given power and authority?

_____
_____
_____

How will you apply this verse to your prayer life so you can begin walking in your spiritual power and authority to live a life of victory?

_____
_____
_____

Day 28
Supernatural Explosive Power

And I pray that he would unveil within you the unlimited riches of his glory and favor until supernatural strength floods your innermost being with his divine might and explosive power. Then, by constantly using your faith, the life of Christ will be released deep inside you, and the resting place of his love will become the very source and root of your life. Ephesians 3:16-17

My treasured child, as you kneel humbly in awe before Me, realize that I am the Father of your Lord, Jesus. I am your perfect Father, and the Father of every father and child in heaven and on the earth. My heart's desire is to unveil within you the unlimited riches of My glory and favor until supernatural strength floods your innermost being with My divine might and explosive power.

I want you to experience the abundance of the rich treasury of My glory to be strengthened and reinforced with mighty power in your inner man by My Holy Spirit who is living in your innermost being and personality.

As you constantly use your faith, the life of Jesus will be released deep inside you, and the resting place of His love will become the source and root of your life. You will be empowered to discover what all My children experience, the great magnitude of the astonishing love of Jesus in all its dimensions.

Prayer - *Father God, thank You, for Jesus. I pray that You would unveil within me the unlimited riches of Your glory and favor until Your supernatural strength floods my innermost being with Your divine might and explosive power. I ask You to increase my faith so the love of Jesus will be released deep inside Me to become the source and root of my life.*

Thoughts to Ponder.

God desires to reveal the unlimited riches of His glory and favor until supernatural strength floods your spirit man with His divine might and explosive power. Realize His love for you is beyond your understanding. It is endless beyond measure, extravagant, enduring, deeply intimate, far-reaching, and inclusive. His love pours into you until you are filled to overflowing with the fullness of God!

Taking Action To Walk In Authority.

What is one thing from this verse God is affirming to you now?
___
___
___

After meditating on this verse, how does it inspire you to take action to walk in your God-given power and authority?
___
___
___

How will you apply this verse to your prayer life so you can begin walking in your spiritual power and authority to live a life of victory?
___
___
___

Day 29

God's Miraculous Energizing Power

Never doubt God's mighty power to work in you and accomplish all this. He will achieve infinitely more than your greatest request, your most unbelievable dream, and exceed your wildest imagination! He will outdo them all, for his miraculous power constantly energizes you. Ephesians 3:20

My greatest desire, sweet child of Mine, is for you to receive revelation knowledge of My mighty power working in you to perfect those things that concern you. Never doubt that I am perfecting you and strengthening you to accomplish all of the plans I have created for you.

Those dreams and desires you have been pondering over the years, I planted those in your heart. I want you to know beyond a shadow of a doubt that I will achieve infinitely more than your greatest request, your most unbelievable dreams, and I will even exceed your wildest imagination!

I promise you that I will outdo them all because My miraculous power is constantly energizing you.

As you experience the love of Jesus, at times it is too great to fully understand or comprehend how magnificently He loves you. However, you will be made complete with all the fullness of life and power that comes from God as you press into His unconditional love and watch your dreams become reality.

Prayer – *Father God, I am thanking You for loving me when I may not have been the most loveable person. I am thanking You for the dreams, desires, and goals You have placed in my heart, and I am confident You will exceed them all. Thank You for Your mighty power energizing me to perfect those things that concern me while I use my faith to stand firm.*

Thoughts to Ponder.

Never doubt in the light what God has told you in the dark. His mighty power is working in you as you release your faith to receive all His goodness. He will achieve infinitely more than your greatest request, your most unbelievable dream, and exceed your wildest imagination! He will outdo them all because His miraculous power constantly energizes you.

Taking Action To Walk In Authority.

What is one thing from this verse God is affirming to you now?
_____
_____
_____

After meditating on this verse, how does it inspire you to take action to walk in your God-given power and authority?
_____
_____
_____

How will you apply this verse to your prayer life so you can begin walking in your spiritual power and authority to live a life of victory?
_____
_____
_____

Day 30
As Jesus Is – So Am I

By living in God, love has been brought to its full expression in us so that we may fearlessly face the day of judgement, because all that Jesus now is, so are we in this world. 1 John 4:17

My beloved child, your relationship with Me reveals that love has been brought to its full expression in you. You are living in love because you are living in Me, and I live through you. It has reached its destiny within you so you may fearlessly face the day of judgement. You can trust in My love for you.

You do not need to hide your face from Me because My Son, Jesus, has already taken your judgement for you. His great love for you is My love for you. You are filled with My love, and the day of judgement is not to be feared.

Rather, you can look forward to it because perfect love has made you completely like Jesus.

Love offers you no reason to fear the future or to fear punishment from Me. Because you are what Jesus is in this world, through grace, you are pure and holy, seated in heaven and glorified. Your faith has transferred His righteousness to you.

When you realize I love you perfectly, right where you are, My perfect love will cast out all fear. I see you just as if I were looking at My Son, Jesus.

Prayer – *Father God, thank You, for the realization that perfect love casts out all fear. I am asking you to give me a greater understanding and a deeper revelation of the fact that You love me unconditionally and I do not need to hide my face from You in fear. Please help me understand that as Jesus is in this world so am I.*

Thoughts to Ponder.

God's love for you is so endless. It is magnificent, so deep, and so wide. Nothing can compare to His love. His love for you is perfect because of the love of Jesus. Everything Jesus is in the earth today; you can be also. Jesus is righteous which means He is in right standing with Father God. Because you are seated in Jesus at the right hand of Father God, you are also righteous.

Taking Action To Walk In Authority.

What is one thing from this verse God is affirming to you now?
___
___
___

After meditating on this verse, how does it inspire you to take action to walk in your God-given power and authority?
___
___
___

How will you apply this verse to your prayer life so you can begin walking in your spiritual power and authority to live a life of victory?
___
___
___

Prayer of Salvation

Pray this prayer to be born again and receive Jesus as your Lord and Savior.

Heavenly Father, I come to you in the Name of Jesus. Your Word says, *"If you openly declare that Jesus is Lord and believe in your heart that God raised him from the dead, you will be saved. For it is by believing in your heart that you are made right with God, and it is by openly declaring your faith that you are saved." Romans 10:9-10 NLT.*

I'm calling on You now Jesus. I openly declare that Jesus is Lord, and I believe in my heart that God raised Him from the dead.

It is that simple. You are now a born-again child of God.

The Bible says, *"If imperfect parents know how to lovingly take care of their children and give them what they need, how much more will the perfect heavenly Father give the Holy Spirit's fullness when his children ask him." Luke 11:13.*

I'm asking You to fill me with the Holy Spirit. Holy Spirit, rise up within me as I praise God. I expect to speak with other tongues as You give me utterance according to Acts 2:4 which says, *"They were all filled and equipped with the Holy Spirit and were inspired to speak in tongues—empowered by the Spirit to speak in languages they had never learned!"*

Now, worship and praise God as you are filled with the Holy Spirit and speak in your heavenly language, or other tongues.

About Lucia M. Claborn

Lucia Claborn is a victory coach, author, and speaker. She helps people who have been hurt by the church, or life, find restoration through building their faith to discover their true identity, so they can walk in victory.

Her heartbeat is to teach people to stand on the Word of God, decree and declare their desired world into existence, and release their faith to receive their heart's desires.

Lucia has been writing for more than 30 years, with her recent books being available on Amazon as well as countless publishing platforms around the world.

Her weekly podcast, Secrets to Victorious Living, encourages listeners around the world by building their faith to walk in victory.

Lucia and her husband Danny live in North Alabama. They have four grown children and three grandchildren.

You can find Lucia online at:
LuciaClaborn.com
Facebook: Lucia Claborn
Instagram: @Lucia.Claborn
Clubhouse: Lucia Claborn – Living A Lifestyle of Victory

Other Products Available From Lucia M. Claborn

Books

English Version

ABC's Of Who I Am – Decreeing Who God Says I Am
ABC's Of Who I Am Journal – Decreeing Who God Says I Am
Your Victory in the Making – 30-Day Devotional

Spanish Version

ABC's De Quien Soy – Decretando Quién Dice Dios Que Soy Yo
ABC's De Quien Soy Diario – Decretando Quién Dice Dios Que Soy
En Vísperas de Tu Victoria – Un Devocional de 30 Días

Podcast

Secrets to Victorious Living
Victory on the Veranda
Listen On Stitcher, Pinterest, iTunes or
your favorite podcast platform.

Course

Hearing The Voice of God

www.ingramcontent.com/pod-product-compliance
Lightning Source LLC
Chambersburg PA
CBHW071840290426
44109CB00017B/1877